DID SARAH LAUGH?

The story about Sarah is taken from Genesis 17-18:15; 21:1-7.

*T**hen the LORD said, "I will surely return to you about this time next year, and Sarah your wife will have a son."*

Now Sarah was listening at the entrance to the tent, which was behind him. Abraham and Sarah were already old and well advanced in years, and Sarah was past the age of childbearing. So Sarah laughed to herself as she thought, "After I am worn out and my master is old, will I now have this pleasure?"

Then the LORD said to Abraham, "Why did Sarah laugh and say, 'Will I really have a child, now that I am old?' Is anything too hard for the LORD? I will return to you at the appointed time next year and Sarah will have a son."

Sarah was afraid, so she lied and said, "I did not laugh."

But he said, "Yes, you did laugh."

Now the LORD was gracious to Sarah as he had said, and the Lord did for Sarah what he had promised. Sarah

became pregnant and bore a son to Abraham in his old age, at the very time God had promised him. Abraham gave the name Isaac to the son Sarah bore him. When his son Isaac was eight days old, Abraham circumcised him, as God commanded him. Abraham was a hundred years old when his son Isaac was born to him.

Sarah said, "God has brought me laughter, and everyone who hears about this will laugh with me." And she added, "Who would have said to Abraham that Sarah would nurse children? Yet I have borne him a son in his old age."

Genesis 17: 10-15; 21: 1-7, NIV

Why Did Sarah Laugh?

Published by Scandinavia Publishing House
Nørregade 32, DK-1165 Copenhagen K.
Tel.: (45) 33140091   Fax: (45) 33320091
E-Mail: scanpub1@post4.tele.dk

Copyright © 1996, Pauline Youd
Copyright © on artwork 1996, Daughters of St. Paul
Original English edition published by Pauline Books & Media,
50 Saint Paul's Avenue, Boston, USA
Scripture quotations are from the Holy Bible, New International Version,
Copyright © 1973, 1978, International Bible Society
Design by Ben Alex
Produced by Scandinavia Publishing House
Printed in Singapore.
ISBN 87 7247 040 2

All rights reserved. No part of this book may be reproduced or utilized
in any form or by any means, electronic or mechanical, including
photocopying, recording, or by any information storage and retrieval
system, without permission in writing from the publisher.

WHY DID SARAH LAUGH?

By Pauline Youd
Illustrated by Elaine Garvin

SCANDINAVIA

Sarah was 89 years old. Her husband, Abraham, was 99 years old. They wanted a baby.
 But they were too old to be parents. They prayed to God for a baby. But God said, "Wait."

One day some visitors came. Sarah made dinner while Abraham talked to the visitors.

Sarah wanted to hear what they said, so she hid behind the tent curtain and listened.

"Sarah will have a baby," one of the visitors said.

Sarah laughed. She knew she was too old to have a baby.

"Why did Sarah laugh?" asked the visitor.
"Is anything too hard for the Lord?"

Abraham came to the tent. He saw Sarah making dinner.
 "I didn't laugh," Sarah lied.
 Abraham went back to the visitors.

"Yes, she did laugh," the visitor said. "But this time next year she will have a baby."

The next year, when Sarah was 90 years old, and Abraham was 100 years old, God said "Yes" to their prayer. Sarah had a baby boy.

Sarah was so happy. And God told Abraham to name the baby Isaac, which means "laughter."

God didn't think Sarah and Abraham were too old to be parents.

Did you ever think something was too hard for God to do? That's what Sarah thought in the story. God wants us to know that he listens to all our prayers. God wants us to know that he answers all our prayers.

But sometimes God says "Wait" when we ask for something. That does not mean God doesn't love us. It does not mean that God can't do what we've asked him to do. It just means that God has something better he wants to give us or do for us. God knows what is best for us! God always does what is best for us!

"Sarah said, 'God has brought me laughter, and everyone who hears about this will laugh with me.' And she added, 'Who would have said to Abraham that Sarah would nurse children? Yet I have borne him a son in his old age.'"

Genesis 21:6-7

WONDER BOOKS
Lessons to learn from 12 Bible characters

God's Love

Self-giving

Prayer Overcomes Fear

Praising God

Prayer Obtains Wisdom

Listening to God

Trust

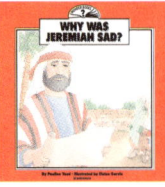
Perseverance

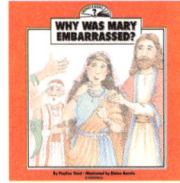
Loving Obedience

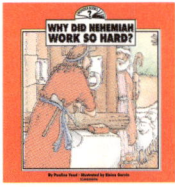
Persistence

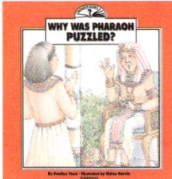
Asking Advice

Trusting God's plan